RECONCILIATION
and Other Stories
and Poems
by Various Authors

What's your story?

Annual Creative Writing Competition
2015 Edition

CreatEng Cafe, Toronto, Canada

Cover illustration by André Gascon
Book design by Emma Dolan
Edited by Jonathan Ryan Vassallo and Summer Fanous

Printed in Canada

CONTENTS

INTRODUCTION

CreatEng Cafe is a community for English as a foreign language learners to get together and express themselves creatively. We have an Inspiration Station, an International Pen Pal Program and every year we host an Annual Creative Writing Competition where contestants have a chance to win prizes and get published.

Reconciliation and Other Stories and Poems is a collection of the winning submissions from the 2015 competition and includes 13 stories and poems submitted by English learners from all around the world. Each submission has been edited and illustrated to create a truly unique and inspiring book.

We believe that creativity can be used to facilitate language acquisition. English learners spend a lot of time focusing on grammar rules and passing English proficiency tests, and CreatEng Cafe gives them an opportunity to take what they have learnt and apply it in a creative way.

Each submission is supplemented with a Teacher's Guide and Student Worksheets so they can be used in the classroom as a learning tool as well. Please visit www.cretengcafe.com to learn more.

This book will motivate and challenge the boundaries of your fluency, and hopefully inspire you to write your own story.

THE ART OF FALLING

BY ILI Z. NORIZAN · ILLUSTRATED BY KIM NGUYEN

THIRD PLACE WINNER

THE ART OF FALLING

They say life is yours for the making
That love is yours for the taking
All you have to do is be bold enough
To go out on a limb
To go to the very edge
Just take that leap of faith
But they forget to tell you
That should you fall
And you most certainly will
You should find the strength within
That 20 seconds of crazy courage
To push yourself back up again
And do it all over again
Like an endless cycle
For that is life
And that is love
Only a circle
No clear beginning
Definitely no end
For where it starts
It loops again for yet another one
What differentiates the first
And the many next to come
Is whether you're brave enough
How well you piece yourself back
From that deafening fall
Or do you crumble
Into refined dust
In the winds

MEET THE AUTHOR

Ili Z. Norizan from Sungai Buloh, Malaysia

I started writing poetry at the age of 15 and have been writing ever since with the hopes of one day seeing my works published. Ultimately, I would like to open a café that serves only good coffee but also reading materials especially in English Literature.

MEET THE ILLUSTRATOR

Kim Nguyen from Toronto, Canada

Born and raised in Canada, however my heart is in traveling to the east. As an illustrator I am inspired by the little things and the cute things. I want to share my kid at heart personality through my artwork and spread a little smile to everyone!

A LETTER TO A STRANGER

BY ILHEM ISSAOUI • ILLUSTRATED BY YASEMIN EZBERCI

A LETTER TO A STRANGER

Dear thenceforward stranger
I have never possessed the ability and art
With which you command language
With which you twist the heart
Mingle feelings and tear the chords of the senses
Relentlessly
And…
Perhaps, never will I
It is a silent night and I have no slightest intention to disturb you
To steal the pillow under your "merciful" "gracious" head
But…
I am a volcano
I am a suppressed pathetic hapless frigid volcano
And each time I dare to speak
Words betray me
Dooms betray me
Time, place, earth, heaven
Even winter
Betray me
And I do know that I shan't be healed
And I do know that you master the art of engraving
Thus
I beg thee
Engrave me…

MEET THE AUTHOR

Ilhem Issaoui from Sidi Bouzid, Tunisia

I am a Tunisian translator and writer of poems and short stories. I graduated last year from the faculty of Arts and Humanities of Sousse. I am deeply infatuated with classic English Literature and its elegance, and I hope to pursue my career as an author.

MEET THE ILLUSTRATOR

Yasemin Ezberci from California, USA

I was born in Turkey in 1985. I studied Computer Animation at Sheridan College in Ontario, Canada. I have been working as an Illustrator/ Designer for 10 years.

NIGHT

BY MAHMOUD NASR · ILLUSTRATED BY ANNIE IDRIS

SECOND PLACE WINNER

NIGHT

"Once upon a time, there lived a big grey wolf. He was gigantic, but despite his fearsome looks, he was immensely kind. He watched over all wolves till the day he died, and even after his tragic death he still watches over us from his throne on the moon, always offering help. All you need to do is just howl at the moon in your moment of need and he will surely help you."

That story was always on her mind. She mostly snickered at the notion of a powerful wolf watching over them, and yet whenever she was caught in a trap or faced the cruel winter, she never failed to look at the bright moon, and then howl pleadingly at it.

She was thinking about that as she watched her young cub miserably moaning. She hoped that her mother's words would be more than just a bedtime story for her young cub was dying. It was a gruesome winter. Most animals hid in their homes, hibernating. Her son was starving, on the brink of death. She was dying from helplessness. She howled every day at the moon. Then when the moon failed to show up, she howled at the stars. She howled for her fellow wolves. She howled day and night and no matter how much she strained herself help always failed to come. She was on her own, and her son had no one but her.

She left him again in that hidden cave. She had to find food for him. She had to hunt again in that piercing cold. She ran, she listened, she watched, panic slowly rising, burning her freezing chest. Her thoughts were frantic. She felt her tears welling up in her eyes and freezing on her face. She had thrown her caution to the howling winds. Death blared in her head, as light slowly receded from all around her.

But then abruptly, she stopped. She heard it clearly—a cry. There she was: ragged, exhausted, and desperate, hearing the sound of hope in a small hushed wailing coming from an alcove inside a giant tree.

She walked silently, holding her breath, and creeping up to that holy sound. This was her son's last hope. She knew she couldn't keep up her search any more, and her son couldn't bear another night like this. She turned to that opening and froze. She watched that little rabbit as it cried for his mother.

She remembered, many winters ago, when she was just a cub; when she saw her first human. He came into the cave holding a blinding light and that deadly weapon her mother had always warned her about. She made terror's horrible acquaintance for the first time that night. She smelled its foul stench as it took hold of her chest, clamping it, and threatening to reduce her into dust. She squealed despite herself, and the human seemed to freeze as if some hidden force struck him. She remembered him staring at her for a few heavy minutes then inexplicably turn away.

She only understood now why he had spared her life: he realized that she was someone's child. He must have been a father himself. It was like some unspoken oath between living beings to never harm a child.

But now as she heard that rabbit's wailing, she saw her son beside him, his chest failing to rise. She realized then what she had to do. She had to be a monster. She lunged forward and brought down her jaws. She felt the heat of blood as it dripped down her face, the smell of it piercing through her muzzle, intoxicating her mind.

She rushed home holding her sin between her teeth, her legs heavy with guilt, and her heart trying to escape her tightening chest refusing to be a part of this crime. Nearing her cave, she heard that dreadful sound of death. She felt the blood rushing from her leg. Somehow she didn't feel the pain, nor did she see her assailant. All she saw were two children, crying for their mothers—and dying alone, in the cold, moonless night.

MEET THE AUTHOR
Mahmoud Nasr from Cairo, Egypt

I'm a fourth-year Med student from Egypt who's trying to be a professional writer. I'm 21 years old. I started writing 2 years ago.

MEET THE ILLUSTRATOR
Annie Idris from Toronto, Canada

I am an Illustrator with a background in Art, Architecture, and Landscape. I draw in various mediums such as acrylic, charcoal, graphite and pastels. However, I enjoy working in ink and watercolours the most. My signature style is whimsical and slightly humorous. The theme of my art is usually based on pop culture and inspirations from my daily life.

RECONCILIATION

BY THIPWALEE SRIMAPHAN · ILLUSTRATED BY ANDRÉ GASCON

FIRST PLACE WINNER

RECONCILIATION

The smell of iced coffee, burnt syrup and roasted duck was pervading the air, as it was lunchtime in this serene, isolated area of a Buddhist temple.

"May you be blessed," said Ajin who had decided to be a permanent member of the Buddhist's monkhood.

The roasted duck with rice and sliced greens was served in a Styrofoam lunch box. This meal was chosen, bought and offered to the monks by Lt. Decha who just returned to his hometown after having spent the last twenty years as a military man in different regions. As he and Ajin were both cousins and former classmates, this lunch was meant to celebrate their reunion.

The monk was impressed by the delicious-looking local cuisine; however, he couldn't start feasting on it immediately, as he noticed Decha was preoccupied with some unidentified activities outside the window.

"Decha." The man didn't seem to have heard him. He seemed completely hypnotized.

"Decha, what is it?" Ajin placed his palm on his cousin's shoulder, gently pulled him back to the constant reality. Confusedly, Decha turned back.

"What's the matter? You've been acting like there's a ghost outside the window."

"Nothing. I..." Decha muttered, "There's something about that kid."

"Huh?"

"The kid who sells pomelos" Decha pointed his index finger out, "Doesn't he remind you of somebody whom we used to know?"

Ajin stood up to tighten his monk robe, and then he stepped beside his cousin.

"Ah..."

"Do you know him?"

Ajin hesitated "Actually, that's Uthai's only son."

Decha stunned, as the unexpected name was mentioned, "Seriously?" The monk nodded.

"Uthai, Uthai..." Decha grinded, "so that bastard has been living in this town for decades!"

"Wait! Decha, where are you going?"

Ajin was obliged to neglect his lunch, as Decha intended to approach the Pomelo Boy. The unpleasant past between his cousin and the boy's father led him to worry.

"Welcome! Welcome, gentlemen! Pomelo!"

At this moment, Lt. Decha was somewhat surprised. The boy whom he previously recognized from the distance was not completely all right.

Ajin noticed the determination that shone through his cousin's dark eyes; it scared him just to think of various difficulties that could possibly be caused by the ire. The man spent 40 Baht buying a pomelo and then he looked right into the kid's crossed eyes.

"Hey, little guy, may I know your name?"

"My name...?" The chubby boy used the back of his hand to wipe away the drool, which kept dropping from his mouth while he exposed a joyful smile, "My name is Kai."

"Nice to meet you, Kai," the older man gave him a hi-five. "It's Monday, right? Shouldn't you be at school?"

"No school." The boy couldn't arrange a long sentence properly. "No school. I work. No money."

"No money? Well, where is your dad then? Don't you have a parent?"

"Daddy's been sick."

"Sick?" The man giggled queerly. "Uthai is sick, really?"

At this point, Ajin interrupted "Come on, man, can't we just let him be?"

Decha ignored his cousin, "Actually, I'm an old friend of your daddy's."

The boy dropped his jaw, "Whoa, seriously?"

"Yeah, I'd love to see him again, though. Is he at home?"

"Decha!"

"Can you take me to Uthai—your daddy? Let's see if we can make him a surprise visit or something?"

Kai was uncertain if he should agree with the stranger until Decha tricked him by saying that he might know the cure for his father's disease.

"I'll go with you." Ajin had no other choice but to accompany him. He had not a single clue of what his cousin planned to do with Uthai and his family, but he knew exactly that Decha tended to be a vengeful man.

In Decha's car, there was the sound of little Kai blowing his nose, the sound of the car's engine and the inescapable silence of unease.

Fortunately, it took only ten minutes from the temple to the shack, which was believed to be Uthai's property.

The dogs began to perform a series of their barking symphony, as Decha parked his gray metallic Toyota Yaris under the shade of the pomelo trees. Ajin told Kai to go ahead inside while he attempted to speak with his cousin.

"What exactly do you plan to achieve here?"

He didn't answer right away.

"Despite whatever you have in mind, I want you to listen to me." The monk spoke composedly, "Time changes, things change; even Uthai is completely different."

Ajin paused, as he wasn't sure if he should elaborate, "The man, whom you're going to meet in that godforsaken shack… He is no longer the guy you used to know."

Decha shrugged, and then chuckled as he drowned in his own thoughts.

Shouldn't he stop hating Uthai? The unforgettable pictures appeared to rewind like an old-school film in the theater of his mind. Back in the old days, when he was too reckless to be concerned about what was wrong and what was right.

There was this boy who played the major role of this film; he'd been known as Uthai. Decha remembered admiring this big, wicked, strong boy, with the same feeling fan boys usually have towards their idols.

The film continued to roll, with the pictures of the two teens spending the years doing all sorts of idiotic things: from smoking to stealing, from stealing to street brawls, from street brawls to senseless vandalizing, which went on and on.

Decha thought they were equally faithful companions up until the point where he ended up as a juvenile delinquent, by a crime he didn't commit.

Uthai was a meth addict and he dumped all the evidence to his ill-fated friend when he was about to be arrested. The boy named Decha was that ill-fated friend. There were also various untold stories behind the scenes, for example, when Uthai started to call him 'Sissy', and talked the whole town into believing that Decha was an actual crack-addict. Whether it was his intention or not, the rumor spread.

By the time Decha returned from juvie to this rural village, he had become notorious. His parents couldn't take it. They were forced to move and ended up with a divorce. Decha was then sent to the troops; his dream of becoming an architect was ceased.

"Are you alright?" Ajin's voice pulled his consciousness back once again.

Decha inhaled. The dryness in his mouth and throat caused him a terrible feeling, not to mention the cross-eyed kid who stared at him through the car's mirror.

"Daddy awake. Get in."

"Are you still going to see him?" asked Ajin.

Decha insisted, "Of course."

"You know, sometimes it's easier to let go of the past and move on with your life." The monk tightened his robe again, before following his stubborn cousin.

Decha and Ajin's nostrils sensed the faint smell of excrement as they entered the ragged shack. It didn't look anything close to a human's house. On a rough mat, next to a pile of what appeared to be garbage, there lied Decha's greatest hate—Uthai, seized by palsy caused by toxicity from destructive drugs. He could only gawk at the visitors with his blood-shot eyes.

It was Ajin who greeted him with a smile, "Good afternoon, Uthai. You remember me, right?"

The ruin of a human being on the mat opened his mouth then made a sound close to 'Uh-uhh', as a sign that he did remember. Ajin gently pushed his cousin, and told him to sit down next to his ex-friend, "Do you remember this guy?"

Decha felt as if his spine was freezing into ice as those drowsy eyes gazed at him.

"It's Decha. He is a military man now. Looks pretty good, right?"

"Ah! Ahhh!" Uthai tried to move as he made a loud noise, probably in joy. Ajin gently touched his hand for encouragement when he tried to say "I...I...r...re..."

"Daddy says he remembers." Kai smiled.

Decha was still stupefied when the scraggy arm of his old mate attempted to reach out for him. And then, out of expectation, Uthai attempted to say, "S....S...Sor...ry". His boney cheek was then covered in tears.

Kai seemed to get confused abruptly, "Why Daddy cry?"

Lt. Decha looked at everyone confusedly, and then, eventually, he tore away the vengeful thoughts of insulting Uthai in front of his entire family, or hitting him in the face with a gun. All he did was bend down, and whispered something to the man whom he used to hate. "It's alright. I..." He almost sobbed, 'I forgive you."

MEET THE AUTHOR
Thipwalee Srimaphan from Chang Mai, Thailand

Thipwalee is originally from the north of Thailand. She has the most amazing mother, boyfriend, and dog. At the age of 24, she is currently aiming to pursue a successful writing career by introducing her work to international readers.

MEET THE ILLUSTRATOR
André Gascon from Niagara, Canada

Born and raised in the Niagara Region of Ontario, André has always been a determined dreamer with a fear of squirrels and dry ice. Co-incidentally he is a freelance Graphic Designer and Illustrator with a passion for anything aesthetically pleasing. André is currently pursuing a degree in Visual Arts at Brock University in St. Catherines, Ontario.

THE SPIRIT OF MUSIC IS...

BY RUTH STEINER • ILLUSTRATED BY R. ERIC DISNEY

THE SPIRIT OF MUSIC IS...

Talking to me like a soul mate when I'm desperate
Healing my wounds when I'm injured
Easing my pain when I'm bleeding

Sailing with me to my harbour when I'm disorientated
Pulling me out of the mud when I'm drowning
Illuminating my heart when I'm disillusioned
Recharging my batteries when I'm running on empty
Immortalizing my memories when I'm dreaming
Toughening me when I'm weak

Opening my mind when I'm blind.
Feeding my soul when I'm hungry

Melting all sorrows when I'm sad
Unscrambling my feelings when I'm puzzled
Scenting like flowers when I'm walking around
Infecting me with enthusiasm when I'm passive
Colouring the world around me when I'm pessimistic

Inviting me to dance when I'm lonely
Salting my life when it's tasteless

MEET THE AUTHOR

Ruth Steiner from Konigswinter, Germany

I was born on September 13th 1967 in Bonn. When I was younger I loved to write. Thanks to my English teacher I rediscovered this passion a few years ago. I live with my husband and my two children in a small village belonging to the town of Konigswinter.

MEET THE ILLUSTRATOR

R. Eric Disney from Kansas City, USA

With 35 years of designing and creating all manner of products for Hallmark Cards Inc., Illustrator Eric Disney comes to the world of free-lance writing and illustration with a passion for bringing an emotional reaction to the people who happen to be recipients of a concept he has brought to life... and what better place than CreatEng Cafe to do that?

CONGRATULATIONS, MR. HAYES

BY AHMAD ABOJARADEH "AA" • ILLUSTRATED BY SAMANTHA HAGGART

CONGRATULATIONS, MR. HAYES

My heart was racing, my eyes closed, and the wind seemed to coalesce around me. My feet pushed off the ground, causing me to jump higher than I've ever jumped before. I soared higher and higher, opening my eyes half way up, and for an instant I smiled. The fear and doubt were no longer in my heart; I was finally flying, if for the first and last time. I landed perfectly on the edge of the window, as if I'd done this my entire life. I was facing outwards and instantly the fear and doubt rushed back into my heart, as a tear rose from the ground and was sucked into my eye.

A vial of pills and a razor instantly rise to meet my hands. I stare at them for a very long time, my heart beating slower and slower by the second. For the longest time I wasn't sure what to do. I have three exits right in front of me, which one should I choose? I walk backwards towards the bathroom, as if some evil force was pulling me back. The closer I get to the bathroom the heavier my heartbeats become. My thoughts race with the wind and the tears are sucked into my eyes more and more.

I place the razor and the vial of pills back gently in their rightful place, and stare at myself in the mirror for the longest time. I hurl myself on the ground moments later, nearly doing a backflip. My tears are sucked into my eyes at a record pace, and I place my face into my arms and hope that I don't drown from the tears. My mind is racing, thoughts of killing myself are coming to me instantly, but as the minutes pass they cool down, and for the longest time all I do is cry.

When all my tears are sucked back into their rightful place I rise instantly, faster than anyone has ever risen before, and step forward, staring at the bathtub before me. She looked so beautiful even then. I check her heartbeat instantly, but it didn't want to be found. I finally notice the gun wound cutting through her magnificent heart and instantly my heart stops.

I only look at her for a second before running backwards out of the bathroom, as if now the room was pulling me towards it. I stand at the doorway; my heart has begun to stop. A moment later I smile, happiness radiating from my body like I know it's radiating off of Elise. "Honey," I say walking back into the living room and walking out of our suite.

I walk back towards the elevator, its magnetic pull telling me I should be down stairs with our guests. As I'm about to reach the elevator a man is pulled forcefully towards our suite. He was smiling, but when he sees me his features darken as we both walk backwards in the opposite direction. Phil, my best man is not very good with words, so instead of saying anything he disappears as the elevator door closes behind me. "Thank you," I say as we begin descending. "Congratulations again, Mr. Hayes."

MEET THE AUTHOR
Ahmad Abojaradeh "AA" from Amman, Jordan

My name is Ahmad. I'm currently studying Mechanical Engineering at WPI in Worcester, Massachusetts, USA. I've been writing since I was 13, and when I'm not writing or doing schoolwork I help raise awareness about mental health and I promote wellness.

MEET THE ILLUSTRATOR
Samantha Haggart from Toronto, Canada

Samantha Haggart is a student at the University of Toronto completing a double major in English and Cinema Studies. She studies national cinemas in their spatiotemporal contexts, as well as film theory. Outside of an academic setting, she works as a photographer and videographer under the moniker CouleurDeFer.

LOLLIPOP LIPS

BY MARIA J. LAZARTE ASPILLAGA • ILLUSTRATED BY NEMO SANDMAN

LOLLIPOP LIPS

I didn't discover I could fly until the summer I turned thirteen. It was a warm humid morning and I had left my house early to walk the fields after a long sleepless night. You see summer air doesn't set well with someone like me with a history of asthma since kindergarten. The moist warm air makes it harder for my lungs to work; most of the time I feel like a toddler or a fat cat is sitting on my chest, like Mr. Gorgeous often did. That night breathing had been an utterly difficult task and sleeping was impossible. I thought that maybe getting out of bed and moving would do me good.

The morning was beautiful, the clouds in the sky were so pink that I wondered if I was really awake or if I had finally fallen asleep and was dreaming of a cotton candy world.

I walked down the cornfields slowly, wishing I had a dog to walk with me. Furry pets and asthma boys are not really a good match. I ran my hand by the crops softly, almost caressing them. The sky reminded me of my little sister's favorite blanket and her cheeks after building a snowman one Sunday morning after church. More than that, it reminded me of Lara's lollipop lips, which I had smelled many many times before but never tasted.

Lara was the prettiest girl in my class. Unlike the other girls she was pretty just the way she was, with her curly red hair up in a pony tail and wearing nothing on her face but lollipop Chap Stick and her black framed glasses. They made her look not only pretty, but smart too, which she also was.

I don't think every boy in my class realized how pretty Lara was and I liked that, it made me feel like I had a better chance with her even when I knew I didn't. Pretty girls don't fall in love with short, skinny boys like me, who like comic books and imaginary sea creatures. They either feel sorry for us or think of us as their awkward little brothers. I was doomed to only smell her lips and think of them while looking at the sunrise on a warm summer day.

I first smelled her lips by accident, in the fifth grade, as she leaned over my desk to help me with a math problem. Almost immediately I became addicted to the sweet and mellow aroma that emanated from her lips. I found all sorts of excuses to get near her: I'd wait in the cafeteria to get behind her in line, or I'd reach out by her side in the library to grab a book I didn't really care for. I was a lip stalker sort of, a scent thief. It felt like I needed to smell her lips as much as I needed oxygen, and God knows I needed oxygen more than anyone I knew.

I tried to find the source of such a magnificent smell many times, hoping to move my addiction away from Lara's lips, afraid I would end up in trouble. I went to many drugstores smelling each of their Chap Stick scents, usually under the suspicious stare of a frowning middle-aged clerk. I found cherry, vanilla, strawberry soda and even coffee beans, but never the lollipop smell I was looking for.

I was daydreaming of Lara's lips that morning when I found out I could fly, or levitate to be more precise. I was walking the fields with my eyes closed breathing in through my nose and exhaling slowly through my mouth like Dr. Reed had taught me many years ago. I was thinking of Lara's lips and how when hit by direct sunlight they looked bright and sparkly, pink and plump; how in the summer days when there were so many fragrances in the air like flowers, newly mowed lawn or the neighbors' barbecue, her lips were still always the predominant smell in any room. I don't know how long I had been walking when I felt that my feet were staring to get lighter. I opened my eyes at once and noticed I was walking on top of the crops, just like that.

I didn't wonder what was happening, which would have been the most obvious reaction, instead I felt the need to go up higher and grab a handful of those cotton candy clouds. I started climbing the air like stairs and as I moved closer I could sense that wonderful smell I longed for. Maybe her lips had been cotton candy all along. What a fool!

I raised my hand and reached for the clouds, when I touched them, they felt moist and soft and melted in my hands. My heart was beating faster with excitement, faster than it had ever beaten before. I breathed in slowly and felt the sweet air fill my lungs completely and then my heart and my mind intoxicated me in a good way, a delightful way. I looked down fearless and was surprised at how small my house looked and how the ducks by the pond had become invisible. I took in one more lungful of that wonderful sweet air and kept climbing pushing myself up weightlessly through the pink clouds; knowing that I was never coming back down.

MEET THE AUTHOR
Maria J. Lazarte Aspillaga from Lima, Peru

Maria is a copywriter from Lima, Peru. She currently lives in Denver, Colorado with her husband where she works in marketing and writes whenever life gives her a little break.

MEET THE ILLUSTRATOR
Nemo Sandman from Paris, France

Film Director, Author, Composer and Illustrator, with broad experience in story making since 1994. He is a true Multimedia Artist, and also a Novelist.

BY QAIS EL-BAKAEIN • ILLUSTRATED BY ANGEL NIEVES

THE FACE OF SPRING

Oh how we wonder
What the future hides
We can't help but ponder
Over the upcoming rides

Who will be the 'Other Half'?
How our life would be?
How much would we laugh?
Will we always be happy?

We all have certain thoughts
About our future spouse
All we need is to connect the dots
To finally reach our dream house

Finding a soul mate comes first
The one to be our truss
To satisfy our never ending thirst
The person to complete us

To be of an appropriate age
To be able to reach out to them
To always be on the same page
That would be the perfect stem

Someone on whom we rely
Entrust with what we think and feel
Whose presence we can't deny
Who's willing to share a meal

Someone responsible enough
One to handle a family
Be able to handle what's tough
And deal with things sensibly

Oh I can go on and on
About the person for the ring
But fulfill those and your heart's gone
For they will be the face of spring

MEET THE AUTHOR

Qais El-Bakaein from Amman, Jordan

I am a 23-year-old Mechanical Engineer from Jordan. Despite the fact that I'm not a big fan of reading I find writing to be a perfect means of expressing myself. Words just flow to convey certain situations or ideas that I come across. Writing is simple and I just love it.

MEET THE ILLUSTRATOR

Angel Nieves from Miami, USA

I have been a Visual Artist since the day I was born. Every cell of my body contains some kind of art and creativity. For the past seven years I have been doing what I love the most (creating art). I consider myself an Artist in different medias. People call me a Designer, Illustrator, Typographer or Painter. I'm proud of the work I've done till today because all I ever try to do is to communicate a massage trough my art.

A STREET CHILD

BY SUPEKSHYA NEUPANE • ILLUSTRATED BY GUILLERMO "MEMO" ARIAS

A STREET CHILD

My life full of tears,
Full of struggles and full of fears,
I work a lot for a penny to earn,
And sleep in the street, not just for fun.

The street where people roam,
Is the only place I can call 'my home'.
The sun and stars are my own,
And the sky is my mom.

I work for hours as a labourer,
But earn a little however,
No one gives me admission to learn,
Oh God! Why am I born?

My parents passed away,
Leaving me alone to go through a long way.
Dad, why didn't you take me with you forever?
Will I not be able to see you again, ever?

Nobody cares for me here,
Nobody comes by near,
But one day I will get there,
Where my appointment is always reserved,
And I am sure I will get all that I deserve...

MEET THE AUTHOR
Supekshya Neupane from Kathmandu, Nepal

I am a fifteen-year-old girl studying in grade nine. I live with my parents and I am a sociable person. I am an enthusiastic person with a good sense of humor. I value relationships and friendship a lot, and I appreciate experiencing new things, writing my feelings and dealing with challenges.

MEET THE ILLUSTRATOR
Guillermo "Memo" Arias from New York, USA

Guillermo "Memo" Arias was born in New York but grew up in Colombia, South America and after high school he came back to New York to go to art school. Constantly transitioning between medias he has been working with art for more than 15 years. His work has been showed in galleries, on the Internet, t-shirts, and the street. His art is usually inspired by his love of history and cultures.

FUTURE

BY BENEDIKTUS GIOVANITO ANTAPUTRA · ILLUSTRATED BY NAJAH KHEMAISSIA

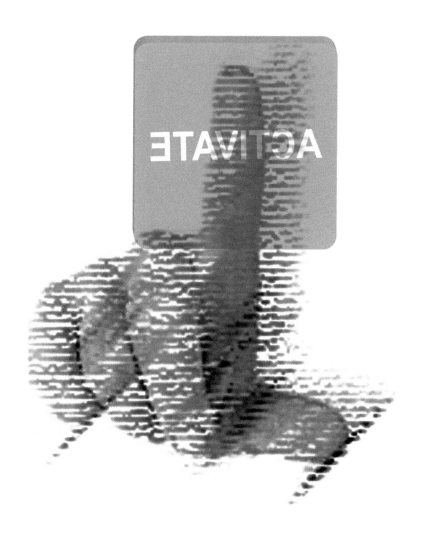

FUTURE

"Jaysun! Rise and shiiiiiineeee!" chirped my ever-cheerful mother as she flew into my room—literally. Great, yet another reminder how much life sucked these days, having had to wake up to this for a whole week straight. Unaware of the dark thunderclouds bristling in my head, she pecked me on the head and rambled on, "Don't forget to eat your breakfast! Today's going to be a BIG day!" she flew out again to harass my other family members, giving me the peace I craved. Well, I thought gloomily to myself, time to go face the world.

Stupid mutations, I thought to myself as I scrambled off the bed looking for clean shorts to wear. Why do I have to live in an age where everyone has superpowers? Now I'm stuck with supercool parents being able to fly and use telekinesis—the 20th century's heaven compared to this life. I suppose it's brought us more good than bad; the Earth was getting worse and worse from over pollution when the mass genetic mutation struck. Luckily, it allowed us to exist on less oxygen, granted us a permanent resilience to harmful UV rays, and most importantly, gave a select few superpowers. Those select few quickly spread to include the whole population. The result is... the Mutant Era.

Kidding, it's not really termed like that (would've been awesome though). Thanks to The Strain, as scientists call it, people were able to develop a deeper awareness and knowledge of nature. Even now, scientists are actually repairing the ozone layer and cleaning air, land and water pollution, a feat our ancestors would've considered impossible.

Thoughts of scientists and mutations were suddenly terminated when a pillow flew at my face. Immediately, a series of snickers ensued.

"Kathe! Karrin! Can't you guys.. erm, girls.. leave me in peace??" I hissed in frustration. The invisible twins are actually not bad until you catch them stealing your stuff. Groaning in frustration, I stomped out of the room knowing full well I won't be safe from harassment until I reach Dad's range of sight. Oh, by the way, my dad has super-sensitive senses; he could actually see the dust rising off the twins' footsteps.

So, after that horrific start of the day, I'm off to school. Here we see why The Strain didn't happen sooner. Super-bullies roamed the hallways before class, looking for fresh meat. Since discipline has been regulated so strictly in our society, that's the only chance they'd get, because when the teachers come in they are expected to be on their best behaviour, or face the consequences. Managing to dodge all of them, I arrived safely in class, just in time for History.

Having pondered everything about the dawn of our era, I began to wonder. Mind you, I'm not a suspicious or paranoid person by nature. I just don't see how a few decades can bring so much change to the environment, our society, and our habits. In 2057, the government finally legalized super-advanced genetic experiments in an effort to fight rapidly increasing infertility rates. Could this 'natural mutation', as the scientists call it, be the result of something else? If that's so, then to what extent has…

"Jaysun Maelstrad! Would you kindly pull your head out of the clouds for a few seconds and bear with us? I would like you to tell us what you know of the 2090s." I have to admit, it took me a few seconds to collect my wits. "Young man, need I remind you that daydreaming isn't one of the gifts this era has bestowed on us? Perhaps if you had been gifted like all the other kids, you might understand the significance of this lesson." Shaking his head, he turned to face the hologram-screen as the whole class doubled over in laughter.

Yup, that's my gift: the ability to do absolutely nothing. I couldn't get back at my siblings exactly because of that. Miserably, I trod home to contemplate my miserable life, accompanied by a drizzle. I had just gone a few metres when I heard a bloodcurdling scream. Sadly, I knew where it came from. Hating the fact that I had nothing better to do, I approached the source of the screaming.

My thoughts were dark as I stepped into the courtyard of a huge, empty building. The sign with the words 'GOVERNMENT PROPERTY - INTRUDERS BEWARE' lay askew on top of the old gate. I easily slipped between a hole in the barbed wire and stopped again. Suddenly, I saw lights up ahead. Instinct took over and I crouched behind a nearby oil barrel. Quick footsteps skidded to a stop right in front of the barrel. I heard the sound of something thrown inside the barrel, then the person raced off.

Long after the light and footsteps are gone, I looked around. Curiosity got the better of me, so I tilted the barrel over, felling it easily. There, nestled on some sticky residue at the bottom was a letter. Quickly, I stored it in my pocket and ran away. No sense coming home this late for nothing. I bravely faced the barrage of questions and punishments handed down by my father, then quickly went up to my room and slammed the door shut.

My heart is burning with curiosity. What's in the letter? I slit the envelope open and found a good old piece of paper. This is what the letter said:

Greetings, unknown person. If you have received this then I am dead. I am the last of the Elder Race - humans of the 20th century. I must pass on this secret; it burns inside of me, and people must know! The Strain is a farce. Somehow, the scientists of this century have accelerated time. Don't ask me how; I am no filthy scientist. What should have been millions of years of evolution has been reduced to mere decades. It is good, yes, but they hadn't yet realized the full extent of their actions. By obliterating those millions of years they have brought the Earth closer to its doom. The meteor Acudalzin, a meteor only recently detected, is supposed to strike the Earth 5 million years from now. The scientists are blinded by their victory and they must be stopped.

I will be brief, time is of the essence. There is a device, a back-up plan that causes our accelerated timeline to revert to its original state 200 years from now. It is hidden deep in a government facility on these coordinates. (Here there is a scribble of numbers.) To prevent future terrorists from hijacking it, the device is designed to only respond to those of my timeline.

You are the last. I wish with all my heart that we could be certain, but the only aspect we Elder Humans retain is this: we remain unchanged by The Strain. I have discovered children are sometimes susceptible as well. Whoever you are, please do this. It is for the greater good.

P.S. the government may try to track down the possessor of this letter. Destroy it.

Suddenly, my doubts disappeared. I could feel the veracity of this unknown person. Now his burden is mine. Luckily, I have been prepared for a quick escape in case of emergencies (that still does not make me paranoid). I destroyed the letter with my holo-razor and grabbed my emergency supply then heading for the window. I took one last look at my dark house then turned around.

Let's just say that the road was rough. The coordinates, mercifully able to be processed by my microcomputer, took me across parks, woods, government areas (I circled around those), and finally led to the border of the city. I tricked the guards by pretending I was a child agent (that trick never fails) and slipped outside for the first time in my life. Dense forests teeming with unfamiliar life forms greeted the eye wherever I looked.

Still, I've come too far to chicken out. I walked across the forest, skirted through swamplands, and played on my microcomputer (not simultaneously of course). I saw and witnessed strange things that day; yet I didn't stop. My goal is straight ahead; it looks like a 20th century theatre. Oh well, I guess it's not that weird.

Once inside the path was simple as the floor tiles glowed when I touched them. They eventually led to a basement. In the center was the device—an archaic-looking computer hooked to incredibly complex machines. There was one button: ACTIVATE.

I thought about it then. Do I really want to go back? Return to a time where natural resources are running low and people destroy nature on a daily basis?

I thought about what the letter said; change is good. I decided, but change must come at its own time. I'll be there, won't I? I hope I get the chance to make a change before this happens again. Grimly, I pressed the button—and hoped.

MEET THE AUTHOR
Benediktus Giovanito Antaputra from Bandung, Indonesia

I am a sleep-deprived 18-year-old currently studying in the twelfth grade. My hobbies involve reading, writing, playing games, and singing in the bathroom. Books began to dominate my life when I studied abroad in Macau. There, my hunger for books (and consequently my English skills) began to grow.

MEET THE ILLUSTRATOR
Najah Khemaissia from Toronto, Canada

I am a Graphic Designer / Illustrator originally from Montreal, Quebec City, where I was inspired by the European style of the city, and the artistic passion of French people, surrounded by Fashion Designers and Artists. I moved to Toronto, Ontario to find more opportunities and work with big names, and yet I am still striving for more.

WILSON, WISH ME LUCK

BY NGUYEN • ILLUSTRATED BY SUZIE MULAGA

WILSON, WISH ME LUCK

2014/12/20

Dear Wilson,

Thank you for writing to me. I love the idea of breaking from technology and writing letters like this but it's not that fast you see. I received your letter the beginning of this month but I hesitated to reply.

I was actually full of anger. A disastrous event has happened to me and I don't know how to get over it really. I was mad, because when I think I'm dying inside, the world seems so normal, like nothing has happened. But things happened right at the happiest moment of my life.

Do you remember the competition I told you about? Did you wish me luck like I told you to? I won first prize! Oh, I know you will be jealous of me. All my family was invited to the last day when they announced the winner. Of course my parents loved it. I succeeded with making them proud.

So right after school ended, I headed to the prize-giving event by bus and waited for my family there. But they didn't come. When the event had ended and I had got my presents and praises as well, they still didn't come. I felt sorry for myself. I stared at other participants who were in their parents' arms and felt sorry for myself. It's ridiculous, don't you think? They should have been there 4 hours ago. They didn't even answer my phone call.

I decided to go home alone after waiting another hour. Walking out of the place with tears on my face, wondering why my family disappeared. Then I saw my uncle. He was standing by the gate, and apparently waiting for me, so I swept my tears away and walked to him. I thought he would give me a big smile and tap my shoulder like my father usually does, but he was crying when I got close to him, at first softly and then harder. Why was he crying? He is always a tough man, someone who even I'm a little bit scared of. All of a sudden, he hugged me tightly and he just hugged me until I couldn't breathe. Then he stopped crying and simply said, "Come with me."

I followed him. We sat quietly in the car. For some reason, I couldn't open my mouth and ask him what had happened. Thirty minutes later, we arrived at a hospital and that was when I started doubting. Something bad, really bad, must have happened, but who, what, where, and why, I didn't know. I kept wondering as my uncle grabbed my hand and brought me to a room where my grandparents, uncles and aunts were standing. They were all looking at some beds. I couldn't think anymore. The door was open and I ran into the room staring at the beds, and laying on them was my family. They looked like they were sleeping, so heavenly, but maybe I had grown up enough to understand that things are not always like they seem. I walked to my father's bed and started crying. I cried because the moment I touched his face, the cold just tried to usurp my hand. I cried so hard my eyes got blurry and I couldn't see anything. Then I started yelling. I couldn't remember exactly but my uncle had to hold me back. I kept crying until there were no tears left to cry.

Some people came and took my family away. I tried desperately to run and stop them. I was insane, right? Sometimes things that seem impossible could be possible in life, and I was hoping having my family back was one of them. I had to let them bring my family away. My father, my mother and my lovely brother, will I ever see them again? No. How could I? They were gone and all the good memories in my life were gone with them.

I remembered the true happiness I felt when I was with my family, when we cooked dinner together, when we slept together, when we laughed and mocked each other. My parents had been my dearest friends, and though it would have been hard to admit, my brother was the person I loved the most. We fought and we hated each other, but then how would my life be like without him? I couldn't dare imagine. I couldn't dare imagine what it would be like if my family no longer existed. And now I have to experience it.

The funeral was held a few days later. My uncle decided that I was too weak and young to do anything, so he stood out as my guardian and helped with everything. I heard people crying, sobbing, saying sorry but my mind was somewhere else. I had no energy left to say thanks, or cry like them. I just sat quietly looking at my family's pictures.

The memorial ceremony went as fast as the funeral. So many people came. I knew everyone loved my parents. My brothers' friends and teachers came. My own friends and teachers came too. They kept walking into the hall until there was no place left to sit or stand. People hugged me, told me that I should be tough and move on, and everything will get better, and many other things.

You may wonder why my family died. I should have told you earlier but my mind hasn't quite settled yet. I am just writing whatever comes to my mind. So, there was a car—a car with a drunken man inside, and he was driving at a high speed. He was unstoppable, and there were no police around to stop him. That mad man stared at the road but looked with blank eyes. That mad man hit my family's car. He hit my family's car without thinking. The accident happened just like that. A drunk driver killed three innocent people. I told my uncle that he must pay for what he did. Things must change, and change forever: he must go to jail and he must pay for what he did. But there is nothing he could do to change the fact that he killed my family. He caused their death and he made me an orphan. There will be a trial, and justice will be sought, but what is lost is lost forever.

I have been back to school for a few days, but I still couldn't bear people's sympathies. I don't want to see them like that. I'm not okay, but life goes on and I still have to live, and I have to live for my whole family. I want them to treat me like usual; so I just give them fake smiles, and tell everyone that I'm all right. The only person I sincerely talk to is my uncle, who I'm temporarily living with, but it's just temporary, because he has a family of his own and I don't want to bother him too much. When everything is done, maybe I will live on my own or something. I don't know yet.

I'm writing this letter with my psychologist sitting next to me. Strange right? I—the one who wants to be a psychologist now needs the help from a psychologist. But she is a great one. The only reason I am writing to you is that she has convinced me to do so, and I have to admit that she is right. Writing to you makes me feel better somehow. Maybe the fact that I can write my thoughts and feelings is proof that I can move on. I know I'm not the only orphan in the world, and I still have grandparents and especially my uncle. I'm still luckier than others. I still have people who care for me.

Thank you so much for spending your time reading my letter. I wish you a Merry Christmas and a Happy New Year. 2015 will be better, right? Love,

Your best friend

p.s. Don't forget to wish me luck.

2015/01/30

Wilson,

Are you back to school yet? I'm in a hurry so I'll write this shortly just to tell you that I have received sponsorship for my upcoming program. After I wrote the last letter to you, my psychologist and I came up with an idea to help orphans in my country. I told my uncle, and he agreed to help as well. Many people want to help us and things are going great. To put it briefly, we will find orphans from all over the country and bring them to a house built from the money we get. I'm really looking forward to it. My family would be proud, right? I hope they like it.

I have to go now, so have a great semester. I will wait for your letter so write me as soon as you can.

Love,

Your best friend

p.s. Don't forget to wish me luck.

MEET THE AUTHOR
Nguyen from Hanoi, Vietnam

I like good books. I like, no, I love smelling them, reading them, enjoying them. I love the world they give me. My life would be miserable without books.

MEET THE ILLUSTRATOR
Suzie Mulaga from Toronto, Canada

I am an Illustrator who primarily creates fashion illustrations in my leisure time to further develop my skills and build a portfolio.

CAN YOU DEAL WITH A CHANGE LIKE THIS?

BY LJUBICA ATANASOVA • ILLUSTRATED BY RIVQUH NAZARETH HORNER

CAN YOU DEAL WITH A CHANGE LIKE THIS?

How many times have you changed since you were born? Sometimes changes are abrupt. Sometimes, you're so tired of not seeing the good in you, and then you give up. You can't pick it all up and start again. You can't be so strong and you can't go against it. No one can, because there are problems without a solution. There are problems that affect you. Still, not everyone can survive the change. But he will. I know he will. Like a novel rose turning its red to black, like a small mouse scared of a cat, he lost himself. He changed. No more rainbows after this rain. Once it starts, it can never finish.

He wanted to avoid it like a young child avoiding the darkness, but he was too wet and too scared. Every single drop was taking him away from the mollifying feeling. Taking him away from his life; away from his children; away from the things he owns; and away from me.

His eyes were now shining from tears, instead of joy. Strong tears; pain tearing his soul and breaking his heart. "It's temporary", Dad was saying, but "he changed," Mom was whispering. I couldn't listen even though I wanted to. My ears were closed; my eyes were looking at nothing but him. My thoughts were away, alone in a desert. My heart is an island, and the cold water is going through my veins, hitting my skin so hard, and making me white.

I saw snowflakes on his hair that were so rare. I saw love in his trembling. I saw sparkles coming out from his mouth when he could hardly breathe. Shadows fitted my memory and I closed my eyes and pretended that he was hugging me. My mind is troubled in my emptiness. Emptiness was destroying me. He was trying to pick the pieces up and make the puzzle - the puzzle of a stolen life, but parts were missing - parts that you can never find again. I pray. I pray for you to feel me again. To be brave is to cry but still to fight on. To be brave is to be you.

As I lay there peacefully beside you, I go back to the days I laughed with you. I miss your care, your help, your support. I hated when you smoked, I hated when you were sad. Your pain brings fire to my brain. I hate those small dots, small dots killing you softly; rampant, raging, they spread like cruel monsters bringing you down. I wish I could fix your bones so you could hug me again. I wish you didn't change. I miss the man who wasn't winded from the punch of the illness, but somehow, I felt strangely grateful for the warning we got. Maybe death is in front of his doorstep, maybe not. Maybe he'll go through it, but changes are forever. As they say, once you go black you can never come back. Go away, silent killer!

Don't make us lose our hope, because those who lose faith lose everything. Who changes for the worse, loses more. But he won't lose this battle. He won't stop fighting. He will deal with the change and start living again. I know he will, because he is my grandfather and I love him.

To my grandfather who got cancer this year and he is still fighting. Everyday spent with him is a gift.

MEET THE AUTHOR
Ljubica Atanasova from Valandovo, Macedonia

As a child, I loved expressing myself. For the past 15 years that passion continued to develop. I reflect my feelings on paper, but I also believe that along with writing, the key to success is dedicating my life to medicine, math and music. I've taken place in many competitions, which motivates me to compete even more.

MEET THE ILLUSTRATOR
Rivquh Nazareth Horner from New York, USA

My name is Rivquh Nazareth Horner. I am originally from Florida and I currently live in New York City. I have been involved in the arts since as long as I can remember. I have developed a background in traditional art skills and I have earned my BFA in Computer Animation. I currently work as an Illustrator, creating both traditional and digital illustrations, and I'm truly passionate about touching lives simply through a work of art.

BLIND LOVE

BY KARIM ASHRAF BAYOUMI • ILLUSTRATED BY CHRISTOPHER POON

BLIND LOVE

The first rays of moonlight began to gallop through the remaining traces of wind, as the misty clouds topped a cold night in the heart of Seattle, painting our shadows onto the wet grass. Emily kept describing how my figure resembled me, and how when I jump, it jumps right with me, and when I wave my hands, it waves along with me. Interestingly, Emily's did the exact same thing.

Emily is the sole person who shares my entire life with me. Our friendship has been intact for a decade after all, but you may be wondering, why would she describe how the shadows looked like anyway? I would answer you if it weren't for the flashbacks that conquer my mind day in and day out, about the accident that rewrote how the rest of my life would go. If only I hadn't decided to challenge mighty nature and rush through the streets so quickly, I wouldn't have been the person seeing with Emily's eyes, or walking with her directions.

However, she has been more than a helping hand to me. I'm surprised she still manages to put up with my constant worries; I never imagined that any living creature could put up with talkative Megan, but oh, Emily was like no other. There was not a single course of hatred that held its place in her innermost heart. Her comforting voice echoed with sympathy and kindness. I was never prouder of anyone more than her. She is my father, my mother, and my eyes; you name it. Her smooth, soft hands were in noticeable contrast to my pale, wretched skin.

"So Em, tomorrow at 9?"

"Yes, don't be late! It's the first day of summer school, just be ready to face egotistical old men showing off their massive efforts in raising the educational standards for many generations."

"Thank god I won't be able to see that!" I replied in mockery.

"True that, but you won't get a taste of the hot dudes either."

"I don't like guys anyway, I am fine by myself."

"Ha ha ha!' She replied in even more of a mockery manner, "this is just something shy girls say, but don't you worry I'll get you looking as fine as me."

"Please don't do that, or else no one will even bother paying us a look."

Our laughs could almost reach the skies, but really, it did not matter. We didn't have to search for fun, because it knocked on our doorsteps as long as we were together.

The golden sunbeams shimmered through the morning and in no time it was the next day. Of course Emily's meticulous attention to detail made us dressed and looking good, according to her, of course, and we got to school in the nick of time. The first class was dull as expected, however, as we were about to leave, I heard someone shout, "WAIT!" and it echoed all around Em and me. A few seconds later, flickers of a dazzling fragrance tinged with a classy scent swiftly tingled my nose as footsteps sounded closer and closer. I could tell there was someone right in our pathway.

"Are you two from town? I think I saw you before," he said in a quiet, yet confident manner.

"Uhh, yeah. Who are you?"

"I'm Miller, but you can call me Mill."

"Mill? Who gave you this name?"

"Granny. Yeah it's a little embarrassing. Anyway, I gotta go now, so we'll catch up later. Megan, I believe? You look good, Megan."

"Oh, me? Thank you. That is nice of you to say." I replied.

"See ya around girls."

"See you, Mill." And he was gone, but the fragrance stayed.

"See, Megs? The guy's totally into you!"

"Em, not interested."

We didn't talk for the rest of the night.

As the days kept whizzing by, we met more often. Of course, Emily is as stubborn as, well, Emily. I knew there were no 'coincidences' and she arranged for me and Miller, or Mill, to talk as much as possible, and as soon as he mentioned his outbursts of passion for animals, I was magnetized. We had something in common. I loved how his eyes saw the true loyalty hidden in these innocent creatures.

"You know, Megs? I feel like humans are the real animals, and animals are the real humans."

"Yes, exactly! I feel like that too!"

A dollop of silence broke into us, until Em rescued the night.

"Maybe one day you can teach Megan how to ride a horse, she tried it once and she ended up with poo on her hands."

"Em! I was young back then, and I couldn't actually see back then."

"What if you got to see the world once more, Megan? What if someone made it possible?" said Mill in a very sincere tone.

"If only," I replied in sarcasm, "It's not as easy as saying it."

I hated myself for saying that. I admit to having liked Miller a little bit, but just a little. There was no way we would ever be what I or Emily picture in our mind. Who wants a blind girl to be his life partner anyway? I should go sleep, and maybe when I wake up I will come back to my senses. I came here to learn, not to love. Love is an illusion to me; just a fantasy desired by everyone.

Two days later all this changed. Here is Miller, telling me there's a person willing to donate his eyes to me. Just like that. I honestly felt like someone else. Chills and goose bumps began to tear up my body. I was electrified. I was just mind-blown! I rushed with him straight to the hospital and surgery was done in a few hours! Mill had arranged all the papers, all the authorizations, and all the other legal stuff. This was frankly the nicest thing to happen in my life, and for the first time ever, I wanted to set my new eyes on him before Em. He was that special. But there awaited a bigger surprise: Miller was also completely blind. His pallor face and luscious skin suggested otherwise, but he was definitely blind. I couldn't absorb what had happened. I felt miserable before meeting him, and now I feel the same way. I wished I never had to see him like that.

"Now, Megan, you finally get to see me. I got you the goldfish you told me about the other day, but I want you to search inside the water for something else," he said.

Of course, I find what I knew I would find, a wedding ring, but something did not seem right. Where in the world of wisdom is it acceptable for me to make such a kind man suffer? No way was I sharing my life with a blind man. His warm, tender heart cannot handle the whims, screams and ness of mine. This is as hurtful to one's heart as a knife, and I cannot go on.

"I am really sorry, Mill. Trust me, you are the nearest person to perfection. I truly loved you for all you had done, but we can stay friends. Friends is fine, so please, let's not be more than friends."

Tears looked like they were racing across his cheeks, slowly rupturing his half smile, almost wanting to drop to the floor as soon as possible. In the moment I closed my eyes he suddenly just left.

And that's it. The love story is no longer a love story, except for one last bit: a week later, there was a letter in my mailbox. Yes, as you guessed, it was from Miller:

'Dear Megan

I still cannot understand why you had done this. However, I have one last wish. Now that you have my eyes, I want you to take care of them, for they meant more than the world to me, because they made it possible for me to see you.'

MEET THE AUTHOR
Karim Ashraf Bayoumi from Cairo, Egypt

I am 17 years old, and I have a deep passion for writing, although Chemistry and Math are my favourite subjects. I have lots of goals, and I always want to do better. I think Egypt has given me great things, and it's my duty to serve my country well and give the world a true image of Egypt.

MEET THE ILLUSTRATOR
Christopher Poon from Toronto, Canada

Chris is an Illustrator, Motion Graphic Artist and Designer. Passionate about the art scene, he attends as many film festivals and exhibitions as his schedule allows. Whenever possible, he contributes his time to the creative scene, by collaborating with local artists of various media, from filmmakers to poets.

CPSIA information can be obtained
at www.ICGtesting.com
Printed in the USA
LVHW050411040419
612929LV00027B/458/P